MA

of the South-West

by Brent Johnson
and Carolyn Thomson-Dans

Department of
Environment and Conservation

Our environment, our future

INTRODUCTION

Australia has a unique and diverse array of wildlife. Unfortunately some species have been lost, while others have declined in number and their distributions have been severely reduced. In Western Australia we have already witnessed the demise of several such animals since European settlement. Many species have suffered from predation by introduced cats and foxes, clearing of habitat and other factors.

In recent times, however, this trend is being arrested. As scientists learn more about endangered species and the factors that have contributed to their decline, action is being taken by nature conservation authorities such as the Department of Environment and Conservation (DEC). Recovery plans for some species are being successfully implemented. Extensive fox control is being undertaken to protect many species and research is being done into other contributing factors.

Exciting discoveries in recent times have shown that our fauna is often able to survive against considerable odds and beyond expectations. Animals such as the dibbler and Gilbert's potoroo have been rediscovered after they were believed for many years to be extinct. Their future survival and recovery now depends on research and appropriate management.

People who enjoy the Western Australian bush and appreciate the living creatures found there have many opportunities to contribute to conservation. Through commercial nature-based tourism, *LANDSCOPE* Expeditions, as DEC volunteers, or as individuals it is now possible to see and experience the wonders of our wildlife first hand and help conserve it.

This book will help you identify the native mammals found in the area south-west of a line between Perth and the Fitzgerald River National Park, east of Albany. It provides ecological information, suggestions on how and where to see the animals in the wild and tells how you can recognise the signs that may indicate their presence. The footprints and droppings are not drawn to scale.

You are encouraged to go out and find these animals yourselves but always protect native bush by observing the dieback and other regulations existing in that area. Don't chase or otherwise upset native animals and leave your dog at home. Most native mammals are nocturnal and therefore difficult to see: stealth increases the chance of a sighting.

Should you encounter one of the rarer mammals in this guide please make a record of your sighting and advise DEC's Wildlife Research Centre on (08) 9405 5100. The date, time and place should be noted, along with any other relevant details.

If you come across an uncommon native animal that has recently died, it may be of value to researchers. If it is not too far gone, place it in a plastic bag and then in the freezer if it cannot be delivered to the nearest DEC office promptly. Should any injured or dead animal have an ear tag then it is probably part of a research or monitoring project and is most definitely important.

Should you find an injured mammal, carefully wrap it in a blanket or jumper and place it in a quiet darkened container such as a cardboard box. Full recovery is possible with the correct care and treatment. Take it to the nearest vet, DEC office or wildlife carer as soon as possible. Phone the WILDCARE Helpline on (08) 9474 9055 for advice. Take care when approaching or handling larger mammals, as they could inflict injury.

Good luck in your search for some of these unique and amazing creatures—an encounter you will not forget.

THE THREAT OF FERAL ANIMALS

Introduced animals have had a major impact on Australia's native fauna. These ferals compete for food, kill and eat native animals and may even alter the habitat required by some species.

Within the south-west, introduced rabbits, wild pigs, sheep and cattle have had considerable impact. Rodents such as the house mouse and black rat successfully compete with native species for food. However, scientists have demonstrated that feral predators, such as the fox and cat, are major contributors to the decline of Australia's native animals.

Feral cats are found across the entire Australian continent and on some offshore islands. They are highly adaptable and inhabit all types of bushland, from cool wet eucalypt forests to hot dry deserts. They are supreme hunters, preying on mammals, lizards, frogs and birds. A single cat can consume up to 20 individual lizards and small mammals in one night's hunting. Unfortunately feral cats are currently difficult to control in the south-west, although promising research trials currently being undertaken by DEC could soon provide a solution. In the meantime, however, it is suggested that residents sterilise domestic cats and limit the opportunity for their pets to hunt or turn wild.

Foxes too have an enormous impact. In the south-west of WA, scientists have shown that when foxes are controlled the numbers of many native species increase. Mammals such as the numbat and woylie have been brought back from the brink of extinction by controlling foxes. Others such as the chuditch, brush wallaby and brush-tailed possum have also increased in number in areas where baiting is undertaken. About 3.9 million hectares of conservation lands across the State are now being regularly baited as part of a massive wildlife recovery program known as *Western Shield*. The baits contain a poison known as 1080 ("ten-eighty"). This substance is found naturally in poison plants native to the south-west. It is harmless to native species but is highly toxic to most introduced animals.

Successful management and reintroduction of native mammals is possible when feral animals are eliminated or controlled. However, baiting is only a temporary measure and research to find a final cure to the fox and cat problem is continuing.

DEC aims to take this work a step further by reintroducing mammals that have long disappeared from the south-west to parts of their

The fox has had a devasting effect on native animals of the south-west.

former range. In its Return to Dryandra project, five marsupials—the bilby, marl, wurrup, mernine and boodie—are breeding in a fenced enclosure that excludes feral predators. New populations of these animals are being released into Dryandra Woodland near Narrogin and other areas of bushland (see pages 66–69).

Not long ago, too many of our native mammals were confined to small, isolated populations. This trend seems to have been arrested and, with a combination of good management and good science, populations are expanding and the future is looking much more promising.

ECHIDNA

(*Tachyglossus aculeatus*)

The echidna is best known for its amazing biology. Like the platypus, this unusual mammal lays eggs and suckles its young. The echidna and platypus are the only members of a primitive group of mammals known as monotremes. Echidnas are toothless and feed almost exclusively on ants and termites. They break open termite nests with their strong forepaws or snout or by digging into soil, then extract the termites with their long, sticky tongues. When disturbed, this slow-moving creature curls into a spiny ball to protect its soft underside, or digs its belly into the soil, so only the spines are exposed.

DESCRIPTION: Long spines cover the body and fur is present between them. Echidnas have a bulbous forehead and a long snout. Their long sticky tongue extends perhaps 17 centimetres beyond the end of the snout. Males have a spur on the ankle of the hind leg but, unlike that of the platypus, it is not venomous.

STATUS AND DISTRIBUTION: Echidnas are widely distributed throughout Australia including Tasmania. Although not commonly seen, they are not considered threatened.

PREFERRED HABITAT: They inhabit any place with a good supply of ants and termites. They live in a wide variety of habitats, from cold mountain peaks to deserts. They hibernate in very cold weather and avoid extreme heat by sheltering in burrows or other refuges.

LIFE HISTORY: Echidnas are usually solitary. However, during the breeding season in July and August they give off a strong smell that may help to attract the opposite sex. Several males may follow a single female in a 'train' until she is ready to mate. About two weeks after mating, a single soft-shelled egg is laid directly into the pouch and hatches after 10 days. Echidnas have no teats, so

the baby clings to specialised hairs in the pouch, and suckles milk oozing from the mother's mammary glands. The initially tiny, hairless young increases its body weight up to 500-fold in the first 45 days of life. It is covered with short spines by the time it leaves the pouch. When it becomes too big and spiky to be carried about, it is placed in a burrow to which the mother returns every five or six days for suckling. Here it remains until about six months old. Dingoes and goannas occasionally eat echidnas. Foxes may be significant predators.

HOW TO SEE THEM: Extensive diggings at the base of termite mounds are a sure sign of their presence. If you notice large excavations under a log while bushwalking, shine a torch inside it to see if the digger is still around. Ant remains are easily distinguished in the distinctive and quite shiny cylindrical droppings.

CHUDITCH

(Dasyurus geoffroii)

Chuditch are mainly active at night, when their white-spotted coat becomes an effective camouflage, matching the dappled light of the moon on the forest floor and breaking up the chuditch outline. These carnivorous marsupials are swift runners and efficient climbers, and can cover a large territory in their search for prey, such as small reptiles, birds, invertebrates and small mammals. Sometimes chuditch show a liking for scraps and rubbish bins at recreation sites in the forest.

DESCRIPTION: The distinctive white spots which cover its body and head make the chuditch fairly easy to distinguish from other species in the bush. The rest of the fur is brown, with lighter shades on the belly. The black brushy tail is unspotted. Its nose is quite pointed and the ears erect and prominent. Adult males reach about 60 centimetres long and weigh approximately one and a half kilograms. The females are generally smaller, at around 55 centimetres, and weigh up to a kilogram.

OTHER NAMES: Western quoll, native cat.

STATUS AND DISTRIBUTION: Once found through most of the southern half of mainland Australia, the chuditch is now confined to the south-west of WA and is classed as vulnerable. The largest populations now survive in the jarrah forest, with

lower numbers in a few areas of remnant vegetation in the Wheatbelt. Whilst foxes have contributed to the species' decline, by way of both predation and competition, it appears that the reduction in range and abundance began before these destructive invaders arrived in WA. A combination of factors such as habitat loss, changed fire regimes, disease and predation

Above: *Adult chuditch*   Below: *Chuditch den log*

probably contributed to its decline. In addition, early settlers waged a shoot-on-sight campaign against the chuditch because of its nightly visits to chook yards in rural areas. However, within the jarrah forest, chuditch populations can increase in areas where foxes are baited. The 1080 meat baits used for this purpose do not harm the chuditch. A recovery plan has been implemented for the chuditch and the species has been reintroduced to parts of its former range as a result of a successful captive breeding program undertaken by Perth Zoo and DEC. Both the reintroduced and existing chuditch populations are being monitored.

PREFERRED HABITAT: Chuditch inhabit jarrah forest and remnant pockets of mallee shrubland in the Wheatbelt.

LIFE HISTORY: Like many other Australian mammals, chuditch do not need drinking water. They breed when about one year old and mate through late autumn to early winter. During this time, the normally territorial individuals will become more active and cover larger distances looking for a mate. The young are only five millimetres long when born and remain clinging to teats in the pouch for about 60 days. Females have six nipples and generally give birth to as many young. When they become too big for the pouch they are deposited in a den (usually a burrow or hollow log) to which the mother frequently returns. Juveniles usually disperse during December and January. The availability of logs and burrows is important for chuditch, as both sexes need many den sites within their home range.

HOW TO SEE THEM: Forest spotlighting may reveal this hunter. If you don't wish to go on your own, DEC runs *Nearer to Nature* activities in the Hills Forest which include regular spotlighting activities. If you are quiet and observant, foraging chuditch are often seen just after dusk around forest recreation sites such as the Nanga Mill area within the Lane-Poole Reserve. *LANDSCOPE* Expeditions are held every year and some may visit areas where chuditch are found.

Photo – Peter Orell

Above: *Baby chuditch*
Below: *Chuditch dropping*

DIBBLER
(Parantechinus apicalis)

The dibbler was believed to be extinct until 1967, when a discovery near Albany sparked new interest in this attractive carnivorous marsupial. Another small population has since been discovered on islands off Jurien and mainland populations have been located in Fitzgerald River National Park. A captive breeding program in conjunction with Perth Zoo has allowed translocations to be undertaken to southern reserves.

DESCRIPTION: About the size of a small rat, the dibbler has coarse brownish-grey fur freckled with white. There are distinctive rings of white fur around the eyes. Another feature is its hairy, tapering tail.

STATUS AND DISTRIBUTION: Though it is now endangered, the dibbler's former range extended from Shark Bay southward and around the coast into South Australia. The dibbler's decline was probably well underway before the fox arrived in WA, indicating that factors such as the feral cat, clearing and altered fire regimes may have contributed. However, even before European settlement the dibbler may have been present only in low numbers. In recent times, dieback has altered the composition of plant communities in some South Coast areas where it once lived and this may also be a factor. Although dibblers are occasionally caught on the coast

between Albany and Esperance, the most secure population is limited to three very small islands near Jurien Bay.

PREFERRED HABITAT: These mammals favour low, dense vegetation with a deep litter layer. Sandy soil may also be preferred.

LIFE HISTORY: Dibblers seek their prey in swift short bursts, often rummaging through leaf

litter in search of insects, lizards and small mammals. They also eat small birds and possibly nectar. While they are occasionally seen during the day, dibblers are generally nocturnal. Breeding on the islands takes place in autumn, with up to eight young dispersing in spring. It was believed that the males there died after the mating period. However, recent research has shown that some males can survive into their second year. Dibblers are thought to nest amongst dense leaf litter and are known to use seabird burrows on the islands.

HOW TO SEE THEM: These mammals are extremely rare and elusive, so any sighting of live or dead dibblers should be immediately reported to DEC.

BRUSH-TAILED PHASCOGALE

(Phascogale species)

Brush-tailed phascogales spend much of their lives in the trees of our south-west forests. These fantastic climbers have no fear of heights, often appearing on the underside of branches 25 metres above the forest floor. The males, however, can only look forward to less than a year of this precarious existence before the stress of mating causes their demise. The Western Australian brush-tailed phascogale is now regarded as a new species, but has not yet been given a scientific name.

DESCRIPTION: This squirrel-like marsupial is grey in colour and has a distinctive black bushy tail. It has a narrow face, large eyes with blue around the iris and large, pointed ears. Adults grow to about 40 centimetres long, with males weighing up to 200 grams and females 140 grams. These tree specialists have long, dexterous toes with sharp claws. The feet are quite flexible, allowing easy climbing up and down trunks and branches.

OTHER NAMES: Wambenger, tuan.

STATUS AND DISTRIBUTION: Phascogales inhabit many forest and woodland areas throughout Australia. The distribution of this marsupial has been significantly reduced by clearing. It has now disappeared from several regions of Australia and become much less abundant in others. It is rare in the eastern States and in WA is

on a priority list of species whose status requires monitoring and review.

PREFERRED HABITAT: In WA, jarrah and mixed jarrah and karri forest are preferred, as long as they have enough older trees to provide the numerous hollows and food source that phascogales require. Large old marri trees are ideal for this purpose.

LIFE HISTORY: Phascogales spend their nights foraging up and down tree trunks. They glean a variety of invertebrates from under the bark and out of cracks and hollows. They occasionally take other small animals. Phascogales are solitary and occupy fairly large territories in which they will have many nest sites. These are usually in hollows high in the canopy. Large trees with many broken limbs provide the best nest sites. Phascogales will come to the ground to move to another tree, and they often cover several kilometres in a night's foraging. During the breeding season, the distances covered by males increase as they search for females. All the males die shortly after a period of intensive mating in June and July. This phenomenon is not uncommon in the family of marsupials to which the phascogale belongs (dasyurids). It appears that an overload of hormones at breeding time can cause ulcers and internal bleeding, ultimately leading to death. This occurrence may be a strategy to reduce competition for food, so that nursing females and dispersing young have a greater chance of survival. Females have up to eight young, which spend about two months in the pouch and are then deposited in a suitable hollow. Juveniles disperse over the summer and breed in their first year. Rearing the young also takes a toll on the adult females and many do not live to the next season.

HOW TO SEE THEM: Spotlighting in forest areas may reveal a phascogale foraging in a tree. A good population exists in the southern jarrah forest to the east of Manjimup. A visit to the Perup Forest Ecology Centre may offer the best chance of seeing this elusive tree dweller.

Droppings

Footprints

RED-TAILED PHASCOGALE

(Phascogale calura)

The attractive red-tailed phascogale is one of our rarest animals. Predation by introduced species, destruction of their habitat by grazing and clearing, and changed burning regimes may have caused their decline.

DESCRIPTION: This mammal looks similar to the brush-tailed phascogale, though somewhat smaller. Its long, slender tail has a black brush on the lower half. Unlike the brush-tailed phascogale, this is distinctively red at the base and the brush is less bushy.

OTHER NAMES: Red-tailed wambenger.

STATUS AND DISTRIBUTION: Red-tailed phascogales were once widely distributed through southern and central Australia, but are now confined to a few bushland remnants in WA's Wheatbelt. They are endangered.

PREFERRED HABITAT: In their remaining habitat in the WA Wheatbelt, red-tailed phascogales live mainly in dense sheoak vegetation, but often nest in hollows of mature wandoo trees.

LIFE HISTORY: Red-tailed phascogales are nocturnal. Extremely good climbers, they spend most of their time in trees, but also feed on the ground. They feed on insects, small mammals such as house mice and small birds. They are in turn eaten by cats and owls. Following a flurry of activity in the mating season in early July, all the male phascogales die from stress.

WHERE TO SEE THEM: They are rarely seen. However, you may see them if you go spotlighting around Boyagin or Tutanning Nature Reserves or Dryandra Woodland in the Wheatbelt. You could also find carcasses of the males in these areas around early July. If so, DEC would like to be notified or receive any specimens.

MARDO

(Antechinus flavipes)

Mardos are small carnivorous marsupials that move in an erratic, darting fashion. They have voracious feeding habits and will enthusiastically bite the fingers of any handler.

DESCRIPTION: While these small marsupials are somewhere between the size of a mouse and small rat, mardos found in WA rarely exceed 50 grams. In the eastern States the fur has some colour variation but in WA mardos tend to be evenly grey with some reddish-brown towards the rump and feet. The belly is usually quite pale. Lighter rings of fur around the eye are also apparent. Mardos have pointed heads with dark, alert eyes and large ears. Their feet have small, sharp claws on dexterous toes. The hind feet are shorter and wider than those of dunnarts.

OTHER NAMES: Yellow-footed antechinus.

STATUS AND DISTRIBUTION: Widespread through the eastern States and in scattered populations in the south-west of WA, the mardo is found in a range of habitats. It can be abundant in some areas and has been known to enter houses and gardens.

PREFERRED HABITAT: The western subspecies is found in jarrah forests, dense undergrowth in karri, woodlands, heath and coastal vegetation along the southern coast. While it was once thought to prefer long unburnt, dense undergrowth, recent studies have shown that the mardo rapidly returns to burnt areas.

LIFE HISTORY: This cheeky marsupial is scansorial, which means that it spends time up trees as well as on the ground. It moves in a rapid, jerky manner when seeking its prey of invertebrates, small mammals, birds and reptiles and may also eat flowers and nectar. Mardos nest in small hollows and crevices. Mating is a fairly

Droppings   *Footprints*

violent affair that takes place in late winter, with up to 12 young born about four weeks later. Like phascogales, all males die shortly after mating.

HOW TO SEE THEM: Spotlighting in forest areas may reveal a mardo, although they are small and difficult to see.

DUNNARTS

(*Sminthopsis* species)

 Little long-tailed dunnarts (*Sminthopsis dolichura*), Gilbert's dunnarts (*S. gilberti*) and grey-bellied dunnarts (*S. griseoventer*) appear very similar. In fact, these three small marsupials were only recognised as separate species in 1984. The distinctive fat-tailed dunnart (*S. crassicaudata*) is also found in the south-west.

DESCRIPTION: Dunnarts are small marsupials about the size of a mouse, weighing up to 20 grams. Their fur is grey above and paler below. Gilbert's dunnart tends to have a whiter underbelly than the others and has white patches behind the ears. Dunnarts have pointed faces, with quite large, bare ears. The tail of the little long-tailed dunnart is longer than the others and is also longer than the length of its head and body. The fat-tailed dunnart has a swollen tail. All have quite elongated rear feet.

STATUS AND DISTRIBUTION: The distributions of the four species overlap. The grey-bellied dunnart is more common toward the South Coast. The little long-tailed dunnart appears in a variety of habitats throughout the south-west, but prefers more semi-arid and arid areas. Gilbert's dunnarts have been recorded in the eastern jarrah forest. Populations fluctuate with seasonal conditions, but none appears to be under any immediate threat.

PREFERRED HABITAT: Dunnarts inhabit areas of woodland, mallee, eastern jarrah forest, shrublands, heaths and grasslands.

LIFE HISTORY: These nocturnal hunters will aggressively tackle prey, often large invertebrates and lizards, subduing them with rapid bites. They breed in spring, with up to eight young becoming independent by January. Dunnarts do not have a distinct male die-off after breeding, but it is rare for a male to live to the next breeding season. These marsupials nest in small hollows within fallen logs, amongst the skirts of grass trees or in clumps of grass.

Above: *Little long-tailed dunnart*   Below: *Gilbert's dunnart*

Above: *Grey-bellied dunnart*   Below: *Fat-tailed dunnart*

NUMBAT

(Myrmecobius fasciatus)

The numbat is WA's mammal emblem, a fact which may have saved the species from extinction. Only a few years ago numbats were critically endangered, but DEC researchers have established new populations and given greater protection to existing populations by baiting for foxes. Numbats are active during the day, and in the few areas where they are found, these delightful creatures are now seen more often.

DESCRIPTION: These termite eaters can be recognised by their slender graceful bodies, which are banded and usually reddish-brown. Their long bushy tails resemble a bottlebrush. Numbats have a narrow, pointed snout, used to extract termites from the soil, and a dark stripe across their eyes. Adults are about 42 centimetres long (including the tail). It is difficult to mistake them for anything else, because of their distinctive appearance and because no other mammals of their size are active during the day.

OTHER NAMES: Banded anteater, walpurti.

STATUS AND DISTRIBUTION: Numbats are vulnerable and now confined to a few small pockets in WA's south-west. They were once found across most of southern Australia, including the desert regions. Predation by the European fox is thought to be the main reason for their decline. Fortunately, the outlook for numbats is gradually improving, as a result of active intervention by DEC.

Following fox control, new populations have been established in various nature reserves and forests. Monitoring and regular fox baiting are also carried out to protect existing populations at Perup and Dryandra and numbats are bred in captivity at Perth Zoo. A new colony has been established in South Australia.

Above: *Adult numbat*   Below: *Numbat digging*

PREFERRED HABITAT: Wandoo woodland is prime habitat. It has the highest concentrations of termites in the south-west and the trees drop many hollow branches, used by numbats as nest sites and refuges. They are also found in nearby powderbark woodland. At Perup, near Manjimup, they live in the jarrah forest, adapting well to areas that have been regenerated after timber harvesting. However, they once inhabited mulga woodland and other habitats, such as spinifex grasslands, in more arid areas.

LIFE HISTORY: Unlike most other Australian marsupials, numbats are active during the day. They feed on termites, consuming up to 20,000 per day, the equivalent of 10 per cent of their body weight. These marsupials dig up the insects' galleries in the soil of the forest floor and lick up the occupants with their long, thin tongues. They shelter in hollow logs that are too narrow for most of their predators to enter. If an enemy invades, numbats can use their rumps, which have extremely thick skin, to plug the hollow. In summer, before the breeding season, male numbats roam a long way from their home range in search of females. Four young are usually born between January and March and stay attached to the teats until they grow fur. When furred, but still unweaned, they are placed in a small underground chamber lined with grass and leaves, at the end of a one to two metre long burrow, while their mother hunts for termites. They are quite active and will play near the nest during her absence. They are able to fend for themselves by October and disperse by the end of the year.

HOW TO SEE THEM: The best places to see wild numbats are at Dryandra Woodland, near Narrogin, and at Perup Forest near Manjimup.

Above: *Young numbats*   Below: *Numbat log*

QUENDA

(Isoodon obesulus)

The quenda can be seen in or near urban areas and even in backyards. In places where human contact is common, such as Honeymoon Pool near Collie, quendas show little fear and can be seen foraging around picnic tables.

DESCRIPTION: Quendas are a similar size to rabbits, although larger males may reach two and a half kilograms. They have large hindquarters but their bodies narrow to a long, pointed snout. The ears are small and rounded. The fur has a coarse feel and is usually dark greyish-brown with yellowish flecks. Quenda tails are short and lightly furred, but many individuals have missing or partly missing tails, possibly as a result of disputes with other quendas. The claws are very long and sturdy. Like those of many other marsupials, the hindfoot has two toes joined together to form a grooming claw. Quendas often move with a distinctive bounding gait.

OTHER NAMES: Southern brown bandicoot.

STATUS AND DISTRIBUTION: The quenda is found in wetter parts of the south-west. It is also found in all eastern States, where it is known as the southern brown bandicoot. Clearing for farmland and, more recently, for urban expansion has considerably reduced its range. The populations on the Swan Coastal Plain are now under threat from new developments.

PREFERRED HABITAT: These mammals are found in a variety

of habitats such as forest, heath and scrubland. They favour areas where the under storey is quite dense, particularly near watercourses and wetlands.

LIFE HISTORY: Quendas obtain much of their food, including bulbs and invertebrates, by digging with their strong claws. These claws are

Photo – Jiri Lochan

also used to construct well-concealed nests, using leaves, grass, earth and other material. They nest in shallow depressions, often amongst fallen debris or low shrubs. Most young are born between winter and summer. Females have a pouch that faces backwards and five or six young may attach to the teats after birth. It is unlikely for more than two or three to survive to weaning—as the young grow and the pouch becomes more crowded one or more of the babies sometimes tumble out, as the mother moves through the dense undergrowth, and are left behind. The young develop rapidly and become independent in about two months. They reach sexual maturity soon afterwards. Females may produce three or four litters in a breeding season. Quendas can live for three or four years.

HOW TO SEE THEM: Quendas are not strictly nocturnal, so it is possible to see them during the day. Dawn and dusk are the best times and spotlighting may be successful. Look for the conical diggings and wait quietly. Good numbers exist in bushland east of Mandurah, particularly near lakes and other wetland areas.

WESTERN RINGTAIL POSSUM

(Pseudocheirus occidentalis)

Ringtail possums are distinguished from larger brushtail possums by their smaller rounded ears, and tails with shorter fur. Once considered a subspecies of the common ringtail possum of eastern Australia, the western ringtail is now placed in a species of its own. This species has suffered a severe decline in recent decades but survives in reasonable numbers in a few coastal areas of peppermint woodland, particularly in areas around Busselton and Albany. However, as the popular holiday town of Busselton continues to expand, the species has less available habitat.

DESCRIPTION: Western ringtails usually have very dark brown fur, with a lighter belly. The tail fur lies flat and ends in a white tip. The tail is prehensile, which means it is curled around branches as an aid in climbing. Ringtail eyes are large and the ears small and rounded. Adults weigh around one kilogram.

STATUS AND DISTRIBUTION: In WA's south-west, ringtails are restricted to coastal areas with numerous peppermint trees and to isolated pockets of jarrah forest near Manjimup. They are now threatened. Their decline, like that of many other mammals, has been attributed to clearing and fox predation.

PREFERRED HABITAT: These possums favour peppermint woodland and jarrah and marri forest with enough older trees to provide nesting hollows. They are also found along rivers in the karri forest.

LIFE HISTORY: Ringtail possums are nocturnal and spend most of their time in the canopy, moving from one tree to another when the branches overlap. There are few hollows in peppermint trees, so ringtails build platforms or

nests, known as dreys. They are unusually sociable and several individuals may live close together. Females may seek the hollows of nearby tuart trees to raise their young. In the jarrah forest they use hollows in the trees and sometimes hollow stumps and logs. Dreys are not constructed in the jarrah forest, perhaps because they offer little protection from warm weather. Leaves, fruit and flowers form the staple diet of the western ringtail. It appears that some ringtail populations can breed all year round and raise more than one litter in that time. Twins are not uncommon. Young stay in the pouch for about 18 weeks and then travel on their mother's back for several more. As many ringtail possums live in close proximity to people, they often nest in roofs. However, people who wish to evict ringtails from their ceilings should block off the possum's access rather than attempt to trap the animal and release it elsewhere. Studies have shown that such animals usually fail to survive the relocation process, perhaps because they are driven out of suitable habitat by more aggressive brushtails and therefore often end up falling victim to foxes.

HOW TO SEE THEM: You could try spotlighting for ringtails in the Busselton district. Look for their dreys in the peppermints. In periods of very hot weather it is not uncommon to discover distressed individuals seeking a cooler resting spot.

Droppings   *Footprints*

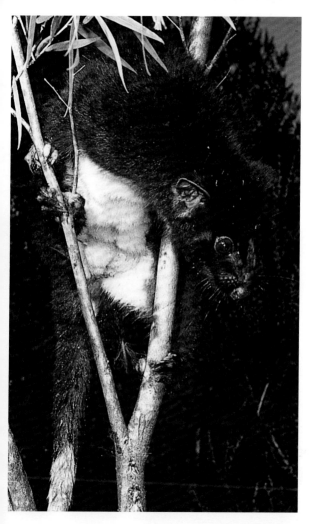

BRUSHTAIL POSSUM

(*Trichosurus vulpecula*)

Brushtail possums are among our most adaptable native mammals, living in a variety of habitats including roofs and chimneys. Abundant over much of Australia, they can survive some disturbance and often flourish when other species struggle. Brushtails were hunted for their pelts in days gone by.

DESCRIPTION: WA brushtails are usually silver grey with a pale belly. Some can be quite dark and occasionally have reddish shoulders and necks. The tail is bushy although the underside is partly bare. The tip can be either black or white. Brushtail possums have large eyes, prominent erect ears and more pointed faces than ringtails. They are also bigger, with females around 1.3 kilograms and males 1.6 kilograms. Males often have a reddish stain on their chest.

STATUS AND DISTRIBUTION: Brushtails live in a wide range of habitats. Throughout their present range they are common and frequently found in towns and cities. However, their former range has been considerably reduced by clearing and they have also disappeared from large areas of more arid country.

PREFERRED HABITAT: They favour open forest and woodland with sufficient older trees to provide hollows.

LIFE HISTORY: Moving at night, brushtails spend some time on the ground moving from tree to tree in search of fresh growth on young trees. Leaves form the main diet, supplemented with fruits and blossoms. They can climb rapidly and make daring leaps between branches of adjacent trees. Hollows in large old and dead trees are used for daytime refuge. Brushtails generally breed in autumn. The single young stays in the pouch for

Photo – Ray Smith

four to five months and remains with its mother for another six to eight weeks, either in the nest or on mum's back. The males scent-mark and actively defend their home range against other males. They are quite vocal and may hiss, cough and scream.

HOW TO SEE THEM: Some people living near bushland, or in some suburbs with numerous trees, need look no further than their gardens. Spotlighting in forest areas is often successful. Daytime visitors to forests should be able to find large marri trees with tell-tale scratching on their bark or large possum tracks.

WESTERN PYGMY-POSSUM

(Cercartetus concinnus)

Those who come into contact with this tiny marsupial cannot help but fall for its endearing looks. Even the most conservative scientists refer to them as "cute".

DESCRIPTION: This miniature possum has soft reddish-brown fur and a pale belly. It has large eyes, large soft ears and a short snout and rarely grows any bigger than a mouse (10 to 15 grams). The prehensile tail is useful in climbing and is often curled. The feet have well-developed pads and are hand-like.

OTHER NAMES: Mundarda.

STATUS AND DISTRIBUTION: Pygmy-possums appear to exist in a range of habitats spread through much of the south-west. Another population is found in the south-east of South Australia. Clearing for rural purposes and urban expansion has destroyed suitable habitat and it is possible that feral predators have had a significant impact. Dieback may also have depleted food resources by reducing the number of flowering plants in certain areas.

PREFERRED HABITAT: Pygmy-possums favour mallee heath, shrublands and forests or woodlands with an understorey of flowering species.

LIFE HISTORY: Although adapted for life amongst small ranches, pygmy-possums will move about on the ground seeking suitable food and nest sites. Their nocturnal hunt for insects,

nectar and flowers is occasionally interrupted by periods of torpor when, in times of cold weather or little food, the possum curls into a tight ball to conserve energy and reduce heat loss. They may nest in small tree hollows, amongst grasstree leaves and in disused birds' nests. Information is patchy, but breeding may be related to seasons or periods of flowering. Up to six babies may be born

and females may have more than one litter per year. The young generally disperse in spring.

HOW TO SEE THEM: This is an elusive animal to find in the bush as it is difficult to pinpoint areas of abundance. Spring visits to areas of flowering heath, banksias or shrubs may turn one up.

HONEY POSSUM
(Tarsipes rostratus)

This tiny marsupial is highly specialised for feeding on nectar and pollen. Its long snout and brush-tipped tongue are perfectly suited for probing flowers. Apart from some bats, the honey possum is the only mammal in the world that feeds exclusively on nectar and pollen. Although they are still common, the plants on which they rely for their food are threatened by the killer dieback disease.

DESCRIPTION: Honey possums are mouse-sized, with a combined head and body length of about 70 millimetres. They have a disproportionately long pointed snout, rounded ears and a very long tail. The brownish-grey fur on the back is usually striped with a darker central band and paler bands on either side.

OTHER NAMES: Noolbenger, honey mouse.

STATUS AND DISTRIBUTION: Honey possums are found only in the south-west of WA but they are common within this area.

PREFERRED HABITAT: They live in heathlands which support a rich assemblage of plant species such as banksias, dryandras, grevilleas, eucalypts and bottlebrushes.

LIFE HISTORY: In hot weather, honey possums are mostly nocturnal. However, in the cooler weather they may be active in the morning and late afternoon. They nest among leaves, in grasstree stems or foliage and even in abandoned birds' nests.

Breeding is closely tied to the flowering patterns of the nectar-producing plants upon which they rely. This amazing species has the smallest newborn young of any mammal but the largest sperm. The testes are suspended in a large scrotum which represents a significant proportion of the animal's body weight. Two to three young are produced in each litter.

WHERE TO SEE THEM: On the South Coast they are occasionally seen feeding on flowering banksias and eucalypts during daylight hours in the cooler months.

GILBERT'S POTOROO

(Potorous tridactylus gilbertii)

In one of the most exciting biological finds of the decade, Gilbert's potoroo was rediscovered by zoology students in November 1994 at Two Peoples Bay Nature Reserve. This primitive relation of kangaroos and wallabies was last recorded some time between 1874 and 1879 and thought to be extinct. Gilbert's potoroo is believed to be a subspecies of the long-nosed potoroo of south-eastern Australia. DEC is closely monitoring the single population and undertaking fox control to protect it. Research into the animal's conservation needs is underway.

DESCRIPTION: The potoroo has quite a round face. Its ears are almost buried in the long, soft fur that covers its whole body, but its eyes provide clear vision of things above and in front, and its front feet are armed with powerful claws for digging. The tail is longer and stouter than that of a bandicoot.

OTHER NAMES: The Aboriginal name is ngil-gyte or gilgyte.

STATUS AND DISTRIBUTION: The only known population of the critically endangered Gilbert's potoroo is at Two Peoples Bay Nature Reserve near Albany. Scientists have been unsuccessful in locating populations elsewhere but a trial translocation of mainland animals to Bald Island has been encouraging.

PREFERRED HABITAT: At Two Peoples Bay, Gilbert's potoroos live in heathland on Mount Gardner, but in the 1860s Gilbert found them in dense thickets of spearwood and vegetation surrounding swamps or streams.

LIFE HISTORY: Gilbert's potoroos dig small holes to obtain truffles (underground fungi), which probably form the bulk of their diet. Like woylies, to which they are closely related, potoroos spread the spores of these fungi, and

Photo – Jiri Lochman

Footprints   *Hopping tracks*

contribute to the health of the bushland (see page 44). They are largely nocturnal but begin to feed at dusk.

WHERE TO SEE THEM: Visitors to Two Peoples Bay Nature Reserve are unlikely to see these secretive creatures.

WOYLIE

(Bettongia penicillata)

This energetic, hopping marsupial is occasionally encountered by surprised forest workers and bushwalkers, as it frantically dashes from cover, mere centimetres from their feet. Woylies had all but disappeared from the bush until research and recovery actions were undertaken, but responded so well to fox reduction that it was removed from the list of threatened species. More recently, its numbers have again crashed, for reasons that are unclear.

DESCRIPTION: Resembling a small wallaby, the woylie is about the size of a rabbit. It is approximately 30 centimetres high, and weighs up to 1.6 kilograms. The fur is yellowish-grey with some reddish-orange tinges, particularly on the tail, which ends in a black crest. The species bounds with head low and tail extended. The hind feet are very long. The forepaws are shorter and equipped with long, curved claws. Woylies are smaller and less rotund than quokkas and lack their wide, flat face.

OTHER NAMES: Brush-tailed bettong.

STATUS AND DISTRIBUTION: The woylie's range has been drastically reduced since European settlement, partly because of clearing for agriculture. It became confined to small, isolated pockets in the south-west, where thick vegetation offered some protection from marauding foxes. Increases in numbers have seen woylies repopulating forest and woodland areas.

PREFERRED HABITAT: This species inhabits forest and woodland with sufficient undergrowth to provide cover and nesting sites, as well as some open areas for feeding. The woylie prefers clumped, relatively open vegetation with sandy soils that are easy to dig. It is rarely found in high

A woylie suckling her young

rainfall areas. This hopping marsupial was once found through much of arid central Australia in a wide variety of habitats.

LIFE HISTORY: At night, woylies forage for bulbs, seeds and insects. Underground fungi form a substantial part of their diet, and spores from the fungus are later excreted. These fungi form associations with plants; they live in plant roots from which they obtain their food and in return they help the plant extract nutrients from the fairly poor soils. So, by spreading the spores of these fungi, woylies make an important contribution to the health of the forests. Nests are fairly elaborate and hidden under zamias, shrubs, grasstrees, fallen logs or other debris on the forest floor. Bark, twigs, grass and leaf litter used to build the nest are carried to the site in the curled tail. Like kangaroos, woylies can carry pouch young while having an embryo in the womb, awaiting birth, at the same time. This means they can produce young year round and throughout their life. They live in the pouch for about 100 days and spend several more weeks at their mother's heel. However, if a female woylie is threatened, she will often eject the young from her pouch, allowing predators to make an easy meal of it. While it may seem harsh for the mother to sacrifice her young to save herself, such behaviour makes good ecological sense. She already has another baby in the womb, and it is preferable for the breeding female to survive, rather than die along with her offspring. The life expectancy of a woylie is between four and six years.

HOW TO SEE THEM: Spotlighting in forest areas east of Manjimup may reveal a woylie. A visit to the Perup Forest Ecology Centre or surrounding forest is likely to be more successful. At Dryandra Woodland, near Narrogin, woylies occasionally visit the settlement.

Above: *Adult woylies* Below: *Woylie digging*

Photo – Brent Johnson

TAMMAR WALLABY
(Macropus eugenii)

The tammar wallaby has the distinction of being the first Australian mammal recorded by a European; it was seen by Pelsaert in 1629, when he was shipwrecked on the Houtman Abrolhos Islands. This Abrolhos population still survives. Fox baiting and the establishment of new populations have helped to improve the numbers and status of this mammal on the mainland.

DESCRIPTION: This small wallaby has grizzled greyish-brown fur, with reddish tinges on its flanks and limbs. It is much larger than a woylie, which can be found in similar habitat, and is more kangaroo-like in appearance.

STATUS AND DISTRIBUTION: Clearing for farmland has considerably reduced its habitat. Mainland populations are now restricted to isolated remnants in WA. These small areas have thick vegetation that provides some protection from feral cats and foxes. Several offshore islands in WA and South Australia have stable populations.

PREFERRED HABITAT: Tammar wallabies shelter in dense, low thickets with nearby grassy areas for feeding.

LIFE HISTORY: Female tammar wallabies are "child brides", becoming sexually mature at nine months while they are still

suckling. They produce a single young once a year and the joey is suckled for eight or nine months before it leaves the pouch. Like other kangaroos, tammar wallabies carry dormant embryos, which result from mating soon after they have given birth. However, unlike most other kangaroos, the embryo does not begin to develop as soon as the pouch is vacated. Males on the other hand, do not mate until two years of age. Tammar wallabies

graze on grass at night but can sometimes be seen at dawn and dusk. Populations on some islands are able to drink sea water without any ill effects.

HOW TO SEE THEM: Wild tammar wallabies can be seen at Garden Island, Tutanning Nature Reserve and Dryandra Woodland in the Wheatbelt, Perup Nature Reserve near Manjimup and Batalling Forest near Collie.

WESTERN BRUSH WALLABY

(Macropus irma)

Brush wallabies are found only in the south-west of WA. They are recognised by their long dark tails. Brush wallabies can be seen in jarrah forest, and occasionally in mallee and heathland, in early morning and late afternoon. They are quite speedy, hopping with head low and tail extended.

DESCRIPTION: Brush wallabies have black hands and feet. The tips of the ears and the end of the tail are also black, and the tail has a crest of black hair. The body is grey and there is a distinct white facial stripe. The young have a faint horizontal stripe on the rump. Their grey colouring is quite different from the grey of other kangaroos and once you become familiar with these mammals you will recognise them immediately from the colour. Males and females are similar, attaining a length of about 1.2 metres.

OTHER NAMES: Black-gloved wallaby.

STATUS AND DISTRIBUTION: Brush wallabies have been declining throughout the south-west over the last 25 years. However, in very recent times there appears to have been a resurgence in their numbers in some forest areas due to fox control. Agricultural clearing and urban expansion around Perth mean they are rarely seen on the coastal plain.

PREFERRED HABITAT: They are most often seen in open forest and woodland.

LIFE HISTORY: Brush wallabies eat grasses and herbs. They produce one joey in about April or May. Their decline over the last two or three decades is thought to be largely due to the European fox, which eats the juvenile animals.

Droppings *Tracks*

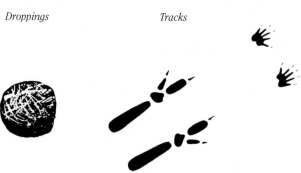

WHERE TO SEE THEM: A spotlighting excursion along the quieter tracks of the forests will usually produce results.

WESTERN GREY KANGAROO

(Macropus fuliginosus)

Western grey kangaroos are great survivors; they are still found even on the outskirts of the city, disappearing only as their habitat is converted to bitumen, buildings and gardens. In built-up areas, golf courses have become one of their last refuges. They can be seen on the fairways around dawn or dusk.

DESCRIPTION: These large, fairly muscular animals are grayish-brown to reddish-brown in colour. The males can grow to more than two metres from head to tail. The females are smaller. Their muzzles have finer hairs than most other kangaroo species.

STATUS AND DISTRIBUTION: Western grey kangaroos are widespread and abundant across southern Australia. In fact, they are now probably found in greater numbers than before European settlement because of the provision of pasture and additional water points. As a result, they are often culled under licence in some areas by farmers concerned about damage to fences and crops.

PREFERRED HABITAT: These 'roos prefer open grasslands, such as paddocks, near water and with nearby forest or woodland.

LIFE HISTORY: Western greys are mainly grass eaters. The males may fight for the attention of a fertile female. They breed throughout the year, although most young are born in summer. They usually produce one joey. Newborns resemble a jelly bean and

take only a few minutes to climb to the pouch and attach themselves to a teat. They leave the pouch at around nine months but continue to suckle for a further nine months, often while another young is occupying the pouch. The mothers and their young use a series of clucking sounds to communicate.

Droppings   *Tracks*

WHERE TO SEE THEM: Western greys can be seen on golf courses in outer Perth suburbs and country areas in early morning or late afternoon. They also inhabit most State forest areas and national parks in the south-west. They are often seen grazing in recently burnt areas.

QUOKKA

(Setonix brachyurus)

Quokkas were one of the first Australian mammals seen by Europeans. In 1658 Dutch mariner Samuel Volckertzoon wrote of sighting "a wild cat" on Rottnest Island. De Vlamingh thought they were a kind of rat and hence named the island "Rottenest" (Dutch for "rat nest") in 1696.

DESCRIPTION: Quokkas have rounded bodies with a short tail and a hunched posture. They have small rounded ears and a wide face that is much more flattened than that of other wallabies.

STATUS AND DISTRIBUTION: Once very common in areas such as the Swan Coastal Plain near Perth and Gingin, quokkas are now uncommon on the mainland and confined to isolated pockets within the south-west corner of WA. They are, however, found at Dwellingup, Jarrahdale, Harvey and Collie, in Stirling Range National Park and along the South Coast to Two Peoples Bay. They occur in large numbers on Rottnest Island, near Perth, and Bald Island, east of Albany.

PREFERRED HABITAT: On the mainland, densely vegetated areas around swamps or streams are preferred. On Rottnest Island, however, they inhabit low and scrubby coastal vegetation where water is not always available year round.

LIFE HISTORY: Quokkas on Rottnest have a well-developed pecking order. The males defend individual spaces and the older

a male is the more authority he has. The males dominate the females and younger quokkas. Defined groups of 25 to 150 adults occupy shared territories, which they rarely leave. They breed once a year, and produce a single joey. Their low numbers on the mainland, compared with relatively large numbers in less than optimum habitat on fox-free Rottnest Island,

Photo – Grant Wardell-Johnson

suggest that mainland populations are heavily predated by foxes.

WHERE TO SEE THEM: To see quokkas in the wild, catch a ferry to Rottnest Island, where they are readily seen during the day.

BATS

Bats are everywhere. Even in suburbia, bat-conscious observers will be able to discern their dark bodies in the night sky.

Eight species of bat are found in south-western Australia. Perhaps the most widespread is the white-striped mastiff-bat. Its almost metallic tik-tik-tik at half second intervals may even be heard in the city centre on summer nights. Mastiff-bats forage over trees and roof tops. They travel very fast and cover huge distances in their nightly feeding forays.

Sometimes in the glow of floodlights around sports grounds, or around streetlights in a well-treed carpark, smaller, more agile bats can be seen dodging and twisting in pursuit of insects. Their dexterity is worth watching, especially when you realise that they are emitting sound pulses well beyond the range that we can hear, and listening for echoes to locate obstacles and food. These little bats include the Gould's wattled bat, chocolate bat, lesser long-eared bat, western long-eared bat, western false pipistrelle, southern mastiff-bat and King River eptesicus. There will often be several species feeding around the lights.

While some tropical bat species live solely in caves, most of those from the south-west roost by day in trees. Many of them will live in small colonies in hollow tree limbs. Some, however, live fairly solitary lives under peeling bark, beneath the skirts of grasstrees or even in dense clusters of leaves.

WHERE TO SEE THEM: Some bats don't fly when it is cold but they can usually be seen on warm summer nights. You could begin by seeing if you can spot bats catching insects in places such as the huge streetlights at the Victoria Park end of the Causeway in Perth. Once you become familiar with their shape and flight movements, try spotting them in parks in your suburb or even in your backyard.

Above: *Gould's wattled bat*   Below: *White-striped mastiff-bat*

WATER-RAT

(Hydromys chrysogaster)

The mainly carnivorous water-rat was prized by early settlers for its fine, dense richly-coloured fur. Water-rats live around lakes, streams and rivers—even occasionally in the metropolitan area. Their presence can be detected by their feeding platforms. These may be on a flat rock or fallen trunk and contain leftover scraps from meals—parts of gilgies, large aquatic insects, mussels, birds and fish. They live in a nest at the end of a tunnel in the lake or river bank, or sometimes in a hollow log.

DESCRIPTION: Water-rats have rounded muzzles and short, rounded ears. They have thick fur which is black to dark grey above and cream to orange beneath. The thick tail is covered with dark hair but usually has a white tip. The back feet are partially webbed. Their nostrils are high on the head.

OTHER NAMES: Rakali.

STATUS AND DISTRIBUTION: In WA, water-rats are on a reserve list of species whose status requires monitoring and review. Their range has contracted due to increasing salinity and pollution in our rivers and lakes. They are found in the south-west of WA and parts of the Pilbara and Kimberley. They are quite widespread in northern and eastern Australia and even occur in New Guinea.

PREFERRED HABITAT: In the south-west they favour permanent fresh or brackish water bodies.

LIFE HISTORY: Water-rats may be active during the day, especially around dusk. They may fight over territories. Females begin to breed at a young age and produce up to five litters of three to four young. They fall victim to cats and birds of prey and the young may also be taken by snakes and large fish.

Above: *Water-rat*
Right: *Typical water-rat habitat on the Murray River*
Below: *Droppings*

Photo – Carolyn Thomson-Dans

WHERE TO SEE THEM: Water-rats inhabit lakes, streams and rivers, especially within State forests of the south-west. Visitors to Lane Poole Reserve near Dwellingup, for instance, should be able to locate their feeding platforms along the Murray River.

OTHER NATIVE RODENTS

 Other native rodents found in the south-west include the bush rat or mootit (*Rattus fuscipes*), the ash-grey mouse or noodji (*Pseudomys albocinereus*), the heath rat or dayang (*P. shortridgei*), the western mouse or walyadji (*P. occidentalis*) and Mitchell's hopping-mouse or pankot (*Notomys mitchellii*). They form a significant proportion of our mammal fauna and are found in almost every type of habitat.

DESCRIPTION: Bush rats vary greatly in size, weighing up to 200 grams. They have soft, greyish-brown coats and look similar to the common, introduced black rat. The belly is creamy grey, while the tail is sparsely furred, has visible rings of scales, and is shorter than the head and body. The tail of the black rat is noticeably longer. The heath rat is quite stout and weighs up to 90 grams. It usually has light brownish-grey fur flecked with black. The blunt face has bulging eyes and dark, hairy ears. The tail is shorter than the head and body. It has dark fur on top with paler fur beneath and less obvious rings of scales—a feature that helps distinguish it from the bush rat. The ash-grey mouse has long, silver-grey fur tinged with fawn and a white belly. The nose, feet and tail are pink. The slender tail is slightly longer than the head and body. The western mouse is slightly bigger than the ash-grey and has black guard hairs over a soft dark grey and buff coat. The long, slender tail has grey fur above and white below. The hind feet are fairly long and the paws are white. The heath rat, ash-grey mouse and western mouse have only two pairs of nipples, whereas true rats have more. Mitchell's hopping-mouse is fawn to dark grey above and grey-white below. It hops on large hind legs. The long tail has a distinctive brush. It can also be distinguished by its long, oval ears.

STATUS AND DISTRIBUTION: The bush rat is the most widespread and common of the five species whereas the heath rat and western mouse are threatened. All have distributions that overlap, but the bush rat lives in a broad range of habitats. The

Above: *Bush rat*   Below: *Ash-grey mouse*

heath rat was thought to require recently burnt heath but has now been found in very old bush near the Fitzgerald River and in Lake Magenta Nature Reserve. The western and ash-grey mice are found in several reserves and bushland areas in the more inland parts of the south-west. Both are sparsely distributed. Mitchell's hopping-mouse inhabits areas east of Albany.

PREFERRED HABITAT: The bush rat lives in areas with a dense understorey, from coastal heath to forest, where it is often most common in gullies. Heath rats are thought to favour dry heathland rich in plant species. The ash-grey mouse inhabits heath, mallee-heath and shrublands on sandy soils and the western mouse prefers long unburnt vegetation of various types, including shrublands, mallee and woodland. Mitchell's hopping-mouse favours sandy shrubland and semi-arid mallee woodland.

LIFE HISTORY: Bush rats produce litters of around five young several times a year. They live in burrows or under debris and fallen logs. These omnivores include a considerable quantity of invertebrates in their diet. Female heath rats are thought to produce their young in spring. They reach sexual maturity at about a year of age and use nests and burrows near the surface. Studies on this species in the eastern States have shown that grass and seeds form most of its diet. The ash-grey mouse breeds around August, producing two to six young, and shelters in complex burrows. It eats mostly plants but this is supplemented with invertebrates in summer. The western mouse has three to four young in spring which disperse before summer. It is communal, with several individuals sharing a burrow system, and eats insects, seeds, flowers, nuts and other plant material. Mitchell's hopping-mouse is sexually mature at about three months, usually breeding in response to favourable conditions. It produces litters of three to four young, which are independent at about five weeks. They live in complex communal burrows up to one and a half metres below the ground.

HOW TO SEE THEM: These secretive nocturnal animals are rarely seen. If your house is near unspoilt bushland it is possible they could be killed and brought in by a cat.

Above: *Heath rat*

Above: *Mitchell's hopping-mouse*   Below: *Western mouse*

Photo – Jiri Lochman

DINGO
(Canis familiaris dingo)

Dingoes were the only dog species found on mainland Australia at the time of European settlement, although they are thought to have been introduced by Asian seafarers as recently as 4000 years ago. Their arrival probably caused the extinction of the thylacine and Tasmanian devil on the mainland. Aboriginal people learnt to use them to hunt animals such as kangaroos, wallabies and possums. Following European settlement, the dingo was regarded as a sheep-killer and was systematically exterminated from many agricultural areas.

DESCRIPTION: These well-proportioned ginger-coloured dogs usually have white-tipped ears and tails, but are occasionally black with tan points. The ears are pointed and the tail is bushy. They may grow almost a metre long and females are smaller than males.

STATUS AND DISTRIBUTION: Dingoes are not threatened but they are by no means as widespread as in the past. For instance, wild dingoes are very rare in the south-west of WA. Their range once extended throughout the entire Australian mainland.

PREFERRED HABITAT: In the south-west, dingoes appear to prefer the boundaries between forest and grasslands or heaths. In arid areas they are widely distributed and density varies with the availability of drinking water, prey and poisoning programs.

LIFE HISTORY: Dingoes may hunt live prey or scavenge dead animals. In arid areas they usually eat rodents and rabbits, but in other parts kangaroos and wallabies form the bulk of their diet. They may form packs which hunt co-operatively, enabling them to catch larger prey than they could catch on their own. The social organisation of these packs is similar to that of wolves. Reptiles

Above: *Dingo*
Right: *Footprints*

and birds are also eaten. Dingoes had a long association with Aboriginal people, and the species has also been domesticated by other Australians. They breed once a year, giving birth to an average of five pups which are hidden in dens. They communicate with other dingoes by howling.

WHERE TO SEE THEM: Sightings of dingoes in the wild are opportunistic. However, they are sometimes active during the day, usually early morning or late afternoon.

BARNA MIA THREATENED ANIMALS

The Barna Mia animal viewing facility is in the centre of the Dryandra Woodland 26 kilometres north-west of Narrogin and less than a two-hour drive south-east of Perth. It provides visitors with a rare opportunity to observe some of WA's most threatened species, up close and in a natural setting.

Following extensive clearing for agriculture throughout the Wheatbelt—and the subsequent introduction of exotic animals— both the number of native animals and the areas they occupy have been greatly reduced. With 93 per cent of land cleared in the south-west Wheatbelt, Dryandra's 28,000 hectares of wandoo woodland, mallet plantation and kwongan is now an island of bushland in a sea of farmland. Its isolation from other animal populations means that restoration of locally extinct species can only occur by translocating species from wild populations, or through releasing offspring from captive breeding programs at Dryandra.

The Barna Mia animal viewing facility provides the rare chance to view five of WA's most threatened species—the marl or western barred bandicoot (*Perameles bougainville*), dalgyte or bilby (*Macrotis lagotis*), boodie or burrowing bettong (*Bettongia lesueur*), wurrup or rufous hare-wallaby (*Lagorchestes hirsutus*) and merrnine or banded hare-wallaby (*Lagostrophus fasciatus*).

WESTERN BARRED BANDICOOT (*Perameles bougainville*)

The name of this delightful animal is derived from two or three darker bands on its rump. The western barred bandicoot has a head and body approximately 20 centimetres long and smaller and more delicate than other bandicoots. The fur is light grey to brownish-grey in colour. It is also called the marl, striped bandicoot or nyemmel.

This bandicoot once occurred in many semi-arid areas of southern Australia. Each animal may have more than one nest,

Western barred bandicoot

consisting of a hemispherical scrape, lined with plant material and excavated beneath a shrub. Western barred bandicoots shelter in these nests during the day and forage for seeds, roots, herbs and small animals such as insects by night. Litters of between one and three young may be born at any time from April to October.

BILBY (*Macrotis lagotis*)

These strikingly attractive and uniquely Australian mammals have long, rabbit-like ears, a long pointed snout and a long black tail, which is white on the latter half. They are covered with soft, bluish-grey fur. Males may grow up to half a metre long, with a tail up to 290 millimetres, but females are smaller. They are also called the dalgyte, rabbit-eared bandicoot, ninu or walpajirri. The bilby once occurred throughout arid and semi-arid Australia, but is now confined to northern deserts, including parts of the Pilbara, the Great Sandy Desert and the Kimberley.

It inhabits open arid country with spinifex grasslands and acacia shrublands, living in burrows which go down in a steep spiral to a depth of around two metres. Bilbies dig burrows wherever they go, and may use several at any one time. The main food items are bulbs and insects such as termites, witchetty grubs and honeypot ants. Bilbies have a high breeding rate in good times and can breed throughout the year, an adaptation which allows them to quickly take advantage of good seasons in the harsh desert environment.

BOODIE (*Bettongia lesueur*)

The boodie is the only member of the kangaroo family that regularly inhabits burrows. This attractive mammal species went from being exceptionally abundant and widespread to becoming completely extinct on the Australian mainland in about 50 years. Boodies are grey, thickset and rounded, with a hunched posture. Their ears are rounded and their tail is quite stout. They are also called the burrowing bettong, Lesueur's rat kangaroo or burrowing rat kangaroo.

Boodies inhabit spinifex grasslands and prefer areas with easily excavated loamy soils. They are highly social, living in complex warrens with numerous entrances and interconnecting passages. Within the warrens are numerous nests padded with grasses. They eat roots, bulbs, fungi, seeds, nuts, termites and fruit, foraging entirely at night. They have a short gestation period and, though they only produce a single joey at a time, they may raise three young in a year.

Above: *Bilby*
Below: *Boodie*

RUFOUS HARE-WALLABY (*Lagorchestes hirsutus*)

The rufous hare-wallaby has all but disappeared from the mainland. It was found across large areas of WA and the Northern Territory and the far north-west of South Australia, where early explorers commented on its abundance.

These mammals are covered with long, soft fur that is greyish-brown above and reddish below. They have a hunched posture. The females, averaging 37.5 centimetres long, are larger than the males, with a combined head and body that is about 33 centimetres long. The long and relatively slender tail is shorter than the body. They are also known as mala or western hare-wallaby.

The nocturnal rufous hare-wallaby was most common in spinifex grasslands of the arid areas. It subsists largely on grasses, herbs and seeds, but occasionally takes insects. It is a favourite food source for Aboriginal people, who devised ingenious methods of capturing it. If conditions are favourable, it can breed at any time of the year.

BANDED HARE-WALLABY (*Lagostrophus fasciatus*)

The banded hare-wallaby was once found across south-western Australia. It has dark grey fur with bands on the rump —the only kangaroo that has this feature. The head and body averages 43 centimetres long, with a tail about 37 centimetres long. It has short front paws and a hunched posture. It is also called the marnine.

The banded hare-wallaby tends to favour open areas with nearby shrub vegetation for shelter. Banded hare-wallabies are generally nocturnal and consume various shrubs and grasses. The males are territorial and often aggressive towards other males. Most young are born in January or February. The mother carries a dormant embryo in her womb that begins to develop if she loses her young prematurely. The joeys spend about six months in the pouch and become independent at nine months.

Above: *Rufous hare-wallaby*   Below: *Banded hare-wallaby*

SIGHTING RECORD

SPECIES	DATE	LOCALITY	REMARKS
echidna			
chuditch *			
dibbler *			
brush-tailed phascogale *			
red-tailed phascogale *			
mardo			
dunnarts			
numbat *			
quenda *			
western ringtail possum			
brushtail possum			
western pygmy-possum			
honey possum			
Gilbert's potoroo *			
woylie *			

SIGHTING RECORD

SPECIES	DATE	LOCALITY	REMARKS
tammar wallaby *			
western brush wallaby			
western grey kangaroo			
quokka **			
bats			
water-rat *			
native rodents			
dingo			
western barred bandicoot			
bilby			
boodie			
rufous hare-wallaby			
banded hare-wallaby			

*If you should see live or dead animals please advise DEC's Wildlife Research Centre on (08) 9405 5100.

**DEC is interested in mainland records only.

INDEX

2007319-1207-7500